BEST BUDDIES

by
Juanita Hamil

TEACH Services, Inc.
PUBLISHING
www.TEACHServices.com • (800) 367-1844

Copyright © 2010 TEACH Services, Inc.
ISBN-13: 978-1-57258-621-5 (Paperback)
Library of Congress Control Number: 2010923811

Cover desigin by Max Stasuyk

TEACH Services, Inc.
PUBLISHING
www.TEACHServices.com • (800) 367-1844

A TRIBUTE TO:

Grandpa Norman and Grandma Ruth who were always doing fun things with the kids.

They loved and cared for those around them and took the best of care of animals big and small.

This is also a tribute to Cousin Benita. All during her life Benita loved Grandpa's and Grandma's farm. She loved Mikey like a brother. Hound Dog and every single animal she ever saw knew her love. Many stray animals lived because of her.

All three of these dear ones eagerly looked forward to a New Earth where all will be happiness forever.

We long to see them again when Jesus comes to give us the perfect home where every day will be a happy day!

TABLE OF CONTENTS

Chapter 1
GRANDPA NORMAN GOES SHOPPING

Just as soon as Grandpa Norman's truck rumbled up to the house and came to a stop, Mikey and Grandma Ruth came running. They wanted to help Grandpa bring in the groceries he'd bought. And you guessed it! They were both eager to see just what Grandpa had bought. Grandma was just as excited as Mikey! Yes, Sir, Grandma was just a grown-up kid!

Before Grandpa had left, Mikey had pleaded, "Please, Grandpa, please bring home some Little Debbie® cakes!"

Grandpa Norman had worked for the Little Debbie® company way down in Tennessee for many years. Whenever an oven wouldn't work, there would be Grandpa Norman getting it to work again.

Now, Grandpa Norman and Grandma Ruth had moved far away and bought a farm with many acres. They missed Tennessee but they loved their Kentucky farm, too.

Five-year-old Mikey wasn't the only one who loved those Little Debbie® cakes.

When Grandma would call, "Dinner's ready. Come and get it!" Grandpa would sit down and just about every time say, "I'm not hungry. I don't think I can eat much." But wouldn't you know it, just about every time Grandpa did sit down he would eat and eat and eat. No one was surprised when Grandpa ate so much. But when the meal had ended Grandpa would often say, "Ruth, do you have something sweet? I just feel like I need something sweet."

Grandma made the most delicious desserts. She made her own chocolate pies piled high with white fluffy meringue on top. She made her own special fried apple pies. And then there was her out-of-this-world blackberry cobbler. She could make so many special desserts. But you know what? It took time to make all those delicious desserts and Grandma had other things to do than to make all those sweets. So, when they opened a Little Debbie® snack cake—it was just the thing! "But don't eat too many sweets," Grandma warned, just one now and then, not for every meal. You don't want to eat these cakes between meals either—only after a meal. That way you eat all the good things for your regular meal, and then you might have a little treat."

Grandma remembered a story she'd heard when she was a little girl. It was about pretending that your stomach could really talk. After you ate something, anything, even the tiniest crumb, your stomach would churn and churn to try to digest that food. Different juices would be added to the stomach to help to digest that food. To digest, meant to break up all those big pieces of food and make them nice and small so they could be made into good blood. Then the good blood could go through all your body to help it to grow as it should.

Poor stomach would work and work for hours, churning and churning and finally it stopped with a sigh. "Whew! That was so much work. I'm so glad that's over and now I can rest!"

But after all that work, could you believe it! Little Mary would see a cookie and decide to take a bite. She thought it was just a little bite. But poor stomach. After all that work it would have to start churning and churning again. Oh-h-h how it ached! It was so tired. It finally had its work done and now it had to start working all over again! "Oh, no, Mary, please, just let me rest until it's mealtime again!" But it was too late! Mary had already gobbled that cookie!

If Mary kept eating between meals her poor stomach would wear itself out. Mary eventually would start having real problems with her stomach and other parts of her body that fed all these juices to help her stomach digest the food. Remember that no matter how little the crumb was the stomach would have to start its work all over again for many hours. So, Grandma learned not to eat between meals and tried to help the kids she taught to wait for their regular meals before they ate.

It would be easy to run into the house when you got home from school and decide to grab something to eat. But if you just remembered to wait until supper, everything would be fine. It was all a matter of getting used to something. If you got used to saying, "No, I'm going to wait until supper" then everytime you said

"No," it would get easier to say, "Yes, I'll go have some fun outside and wait for Grandma or Mom to make a good meal for me."

Of course, there are some boys and girls who do have some big problems and the doctor has said they need to eat more often. But unless the doctor says you need to eat more often, those in-between-meal snacks would make the problem even bigger.

So, anyway, today Grandpa was happy to get some cakes, especially when Mikey had asked him nicely if he could get them.

There were so many different kinds to choose from. They loved the big oatmeal cookies (they called them Oatmeal Creme Pies®) with soft white icing between them. The chocolate Swiss Rolls®, rolled like Jelly Rolls with white icing in them, were so yummy! The Nutty Bars® with peanut butter inside and chocolate coating were so delicious! And there were so many other snack cakes that it was really hard to choose which ones to bring home this time. So, usually you bought several boxes of snack cakes. Mikey was so eager to see what Grandpa Norman bought today! But first he and Grandma wanted to help Grandpa get those groceries inside.

Best Buddies

Chapter 2

GRANDPA'S SACK OF POTATOES

Grandpa had a big smile on his face. He was carrying something that looked like a big sack of potatoes. But when Mikey ran up to Grandpa, that "big sack of potatoes" looked up at Mikey with these big bright eyes and wiggled his ears. He looked scared! But when he looked into Mikey's big, bright, smiling eyes he felt like Mikey was a friend!

When Grandpa first saw him he didn't seem to be the smartest of the litter. He just kind of hung back in his own corner this day that Grandpa Norman picked him out. But someway he looked at Grandpa with just the right look and soon he was swooped up.

Grandpa was so high off the ground—probably six floors high for a puppy his size—if you could build a puppy apartment house. The little puppy's feet were dangling and his ears went flat as he trembled for fear he'd be dropped as Grandpa tried to balance his pink, fat, puppy tummy on his arm. The truck ride was scary! He had no earthly idea where he was. He wondered why his mother and his brothers and sisters weren't around.

He started to whine but Grandpa stroked his fur and spoke soft words to him and he stuck his nose under Grandpa's arm. Someway he seemed to know that Grandpa was a kind man but things were so strange! But soon he fell asleep and seemed to like the purring of the truck's motor.

"Grandpa, I didn't know you were going to get a puppy. Can we have him for keeps?" Mikey was so excited.

"This man was outside the grocery store trying to find good homes for all his puppies." Grandpa said. "All of a sudden I decided, 'We need a dog for our farm. We need a playmate for

Mikey!' And this one just looked up at me like he said, 'Take me!'"

Grandpa named the puppy Pougie. Pougie was a little, light tan puppy. His fur was so soft and fuzzy. And his little pink tongue tried to tell you in the only way he knew how, "I love you," as he licked your hand, your arm, and even your face! Now, as he looked up at Mikey's big blue eyes and big smile on his face he gave Mikey a big slurpy kiss right on his mouth. And that was it. They stole each other's hearts. They would be close buddies forever!

Pougie's mom was a collie and his dad was a German shepherd, but he looked neither like his mom nor his dad. In fact, he just looked like himself—a fuzzy, light brown puppy! His little pink tummy was so fat! He had big paws. Most people said when a puppy has big paws he's going to grow to be a BIG dog!

Grandpa let Mikey hold Pougie while he got some boards and made a little yard for Pougie to stay in until he got bigger. He gave him some food scraps from the table and some soft cloths for a bed and soon Pougie did what most puppies do—he fell fast asleep! But he'd wake up now and then and whine to say he was lonesome and missed all his doggie family

When Mikey heard Pougie whine he'd be right there, step over the boards and hold Pougie close. Mikey knew what it was like to be lonesome. When his mom first brought him to stay with Grandpa and Grandma he was so happy. He loved them and he loved their farm. But when his mom told him, "I've got to go to work to try to make some money for us but for now I'm going to leave you with Grandma and Grandpa while I'm away at work," he didn't know just what all that meant and looked kind of sad. "But I'll come back to see you sometimes." That night Mikey felt so lonesome. He wasn't in his own bed. But as the days went by he had so much fun and once more had his own bed. He forgot about being lonesome.

So, when Mikey heard Pougie whine, he held him close and promised him that soon he wouldn't be lonesome any more.

But Grandpa didn't know just how smart Pougie would be! Soon Pougie began to watch Mikey go over the boards and it was as if he said, "If he can do it, so can I!" He felt like he was in prison. He knew there was a big world outside of this pen and he was determined to get there.

Pougie began to scratch and scratch at the boards and jump and jump as high as he could go. Before long his big front paws caught on the top edge of the boards. His fat tummy balanced on the top and then his

19

hind legs followed his tummy as he fell over the boards! Ah! Yes, there WAS a big world out there—a big world he wanted to explore. Grandpa and Mikey were surprised when little Pougie met them at the door. Grandpa realized that Pougie wasn't meant to be in a pen. He had acres and acres to roam but for now Pougie would follow Grandpa and Mikey all around.

Grandpa loved to feed his cows and horses in the big barn. As Grandpa milked the cows he poured some nice warm milk into a little pan. Pougie's little pink tongue lapped up the warm milk. It felt so good going down his throat and into his tummy. Soon Pougie's little pink tummy looked like a big balloon that was ready to pop. Then Pougie found a nice warm spot where the sun beamed down and did what most puppies do—he fell sound asleep.

It didn't take long for a little Banti rooster to discover that some animal was in his yard that he'd never seen before. The rooster squawked and squawked at Pougie but when Pougie didn't try to catch the little golden rooster he soon went away to scratch for worms.

Daisy the soft-haired, brown, Jersey cow lowered her head to the ground and glared with her big black eyes at this new animal. She made a run at Pougie but when Pougie got out of the way she decided that Pougie wasn't an enemy after all.

After a few days of following Grandpa and Mikey around, the puppy days of sleep turned into days of investigation. Pougie wanted to see what this big world was all about. Each day he'd go a little bit further from the house. His nose twitched as he caught the scent of another wild animal and there were so many.

Pougie grew fast—he knew he was loved—and he knew this was his family and his place. He would protect his family and the farm with all his might.

A creek, long and wide, ran through the farm. Little springs and big springs—all of them cold springs trickled down into the creek.

When you waded in the creek or swam in the creek it was always cold. You had to get used to the cold water for a bit until you felt warm enough to swim.

Many families loved to come to this creek, especially where one particular place was wide enough and deep enough to call the old swimmin' hole. Many days you would hear people splashing around, yelling and enjoying the old swimmin' hole. Soon Pougie learned who belonged there.

At night when the family was fast asleep Pougie would hear the night animals wake up. The big bright moon made the night look almost like day. Down by the creek he'd hear a raccoon and its family. He'd sneak up to watch them down by the creek as they washed the ears of corn they'd stolen from Grandpa's corn patch.

Coons always liked to wash their food before they ate it, just like Grandma tried to teach Mikey to always wash his hands before he ate.

Coons are known to be brave and often when a dog comes after them in the water they will duck the dog's head under the water to protect themselves. But Grandpa soon learned that the puppy Pougie was indeed a smart dog. He grew so strong and so smart that Grandpa began to call him Hound Dog instead of by his puppy name. Hound Dog outsmarted the coons and never got caught. He chased them away from Grandpa's corn patch.

There were neat little animal trails on the far bank of the creek over the rock layers and under the Mountain Laurel bushes that hung over the trails. In the springtime Hound Dog spread the pretty pink blossoms of the Mountain Laurels over these trails as he ran under the bushes that hung over the rocks.

Grandma and Grandpa and Mikey would often sit on the porch at night and hear the fox's raspy bark. Soon Mikey easily learned the difference between a fox bark and a dog bark. Hound Dog's sharp ears heard the fox barks and before you knew it he'd leave Grandma, Grandpa, and Mikey far behind as he was off on a fox hunt.

The big, fat chickens liked to roost on the chicken roosts. The roosting poles were big, round poles Grandpa made for them and placed them far off the ground in the barn. But the little Bantum chickens, they called

"Banti" chickens didn't like to stay in the barn or a chicken house. They loved to roost in the trees around the house. Hound Dog kept the foxes far away from the chicken roosts and Grandpa and Grandma felt very lucky for their faithful Hound Dog. Of all the dogs they'd ever had Hound Dog was the very smartest, most loving, and most faithful of all!

Sometimes a big opossum would come near the house. Hound Dog would run to the possum and bark and bark to let Grandpa know some strange animal was near. The possum would open its mouth showing that mouthful of many sharp teeth but Hound Dog wasn't afraid of all those teeth. He'd continue to nip at the possum's tail until Grandpa came to see what all the commotion was about.

Sometimes a snake would slither around the chickens. Snakes liked chickens and their eggs. But Hound

Dog would chase the snakes away. Mikey liked playing with the snakes.

Grandpa could just about tell what animal was around just by the way Hound Dog barked and carried on. Opossums love chickens and eggs. The Banti chickens not only liked to roost in trees but they also liked to sneak out somewhere outside of the barn and lay their eggs in a nest that they made in the grass. So, every day Mikey had an Easter egg hunt as he tried to find the hen nests. You never knew where a new nest would be. But of course, when they made their nests they would often lay many eggs in the same nest and sit on those eggs until the baby chickens hatched. So there were chickens roosting in the trees and then there were mama chickens sitting on their nests of eggs. Any possum or fox would love to find these.

Mikey soon learned that the big, fat, black and white chickens had little black chicks. The big, fat, red chickens and white chickens had little yellow chicks. But the little Banti chickens had tiny yellow chicks with brown stripes on their heads and little wings.

No matter what color they were Mikey loved little chicks. He tried to make sure they were safe. And, of course, Hound Dog did the same. It wasn't true that all farm dogs protected chickens. You usually had to get rid of a dog that liked to suck eggs or one that liked to catch and eat chickens but Hound Dog was never that kind of dog.

Mikey sometimes would sit and sit waiting as long as he could to see a hen lay an egg. And then after he found a whole nest of eggs he'd tell Grandma or Grandpa where the nest was. The mama hen would squawk and squawk at Mikey and fluff her wings out trying to scare him away. If he got too close she would peck him fiercely. He learned to stay away from a "settin' hen." An old mama hen could flog and flog, beating hard with her wings. God taught her to take care of her little ones.

But when Mikey would tell Grandma or Grandpa he'd found a settin' hen they would make a chicken coop for the nesting mama hen.

They'd make these coops by crisscrossing sticks until they made a pyramid, getting smaller at the top. They'd lay a couple of boards over the top so they could reach in to feed the hen. During the day they could open the top of the coop so that Mama hen could go in and out to do what she needed to do. She always knew where her eggs were and came right back when she was ready. She didn't want to leave her eggs long. She wanted to keep them warm so that the babies inside the eggs would grow as they should.

A few years back there was a fire in the neighborhood. It all started when a man accidently poured gasoline, instead of kerosene, on the wood in the fireplace to get it started. Then when he lit the wood, all of a sudden the flames whooshed up the chimney and all through the room. The whole house was on fire!

But when the fire went out they found a mother hen on her nest. The family had made a nest in a box and brought Mama Hen and her baby chicks inside the kitchen so they'd be safe from the cold weather.

Mama Hen could have flown away but she stayed on her nest to take care of her chicks. Brave Mama Hen died from all the smoke but underneath her wings, all snuggled safe, were her baby chicks all alive!

Grandma remembered the story in the Bible when Jesus was talking to the people in the city of Jerusalem. With tears in His eyes, and a heart full of love, He told them that He often longed to gather them under His wings like a mother hen, but they wouldn't let Him! Like Brave Mama Hen He had tried His best to save the people in Jerusalem but they wouldn't listen. They thought they knew best.

While they sat in the porch swing in the evening Mikey asked Grandma to tell him stories before he went to bed.

Chapter 3
CRITTERS BIG AND SMALL

When Grandma heard the fox barking it reminded her of the story of a boy named Jesus who lived many long years before.

Jesus, like Mikey, loved all animals. He probably had a favorite faithful dog like Hound Dog. In fact, Jesus actually made all the animals.

When God planned to make this world He wanted it filled with beautiful things to make it a happy place for us. His son, Jesus, was assigned to make all the interesting animals for us to enjoy,

Jesus must have had a lot of fun making the different kinds of animals. He made the tiny mouse to wiggle its whiskers and the big fat elephant to use its trunk like a water hose to squirt water. He made the funny monkey to hang by it's tail and make funny noises.

Some animals had huge mouths like the hippo and some had long necks like the giraffe.

Some animals were made with short legs, some with long legs; some were made with long ears while others were made with small ears. What a lot of fun Jesus must have had making all these animals! He must have laughed as He thought of how He wanted our world to be a happy place to live!

He made all kinds of different birds and fish. There was the big eagle and the tiny, tiny hummingbird. Some birds had big, colorful bills like the puffin, and spoonbill, and the toucan. Other birds had tiny, sharp bills.

There was the huge whale and the tiny goldfish. Grandma bought Mikey a bowl with little goldfish. Mikey loved to watch the goldfish gulp and look at him with their big eyes. He learned to take care of his fish and feed them every day.

No matter how Mikey would take a piece of clay and try to make a really neat animal or a bird, he just couldn't make them live. Only Jesus could make an animal breathe and see through its eyes, move around and really live! Only Jesus could make a bird fly!

Jesus came down from a beautiful, wonderful, peaceful home, down, down to this earth as a baby just like Mikey was a baby. His mom and dad loved Him so very much and tried to teach Him to always be kind and loving to His animals and all His friends. But the brothers of Jesus and most of His friends really didn't understand Him. They didn't know why He wanted to always be so good. They wanted Him to join in with them as they sometimes teased their friends and made them feel bad.

Just because Jesus was so good they called him names like "Goody, two shoes!" They knew they weren't doing right but because He wouldn't join them in doing wrong they felt like He was saying they were bad. They thought maybe He would even tell their moms and dads about the bad things they did. So, Jesus often felt alone and was often misunderstood,

When Jesus grew to be a grown man, the people around Him who had grown up still doing bad things started telling things about Him that weren't true. They even went so far as to nail Him to a cross. That was such a cruel and painful thing to do to a person! While Jesus was hanging on the cross between Heaven and Earth He begged God to forgive them, saying that they really didn't know what they were doing. Jesus' heart was always so full of love. No one on earth ever loved anyone as much as Jesus loved them.

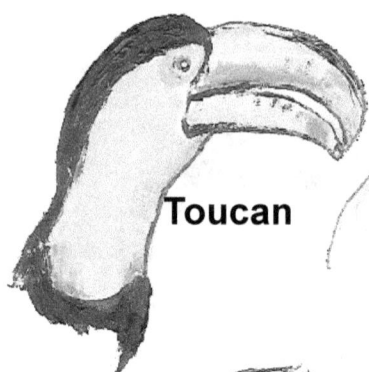

Toucan

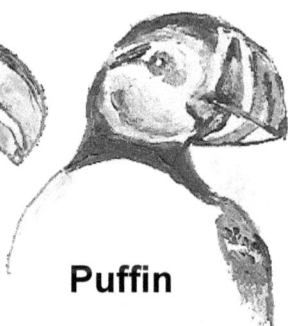

Puffin

Pelican

Hornbill

Hummingbird

Dominecker

Banti

God had said that anyone who sinned would have to pay for their sins; they would have to die. He never wanted the good children to have to live in a world where they would be so sad when bad people did or said things to them that hurt them so badly. But Jesus said, "If someone does something wrong and really, truly is sorry, let me die for their sins so that they don't have to die! Let me take their place!"

God knew that this was the only way people could have their sins paid for. Only someone who had never sinned could take the place of another person who asked for forgiveness. He knew that there was only one person who could give His life to pay for their sins.

God's heart broke as He thought of sending Jesus far away from His loving home so that He could show all the people in the world the love that God had for them and how to live a good life.

God's heart was so heavy with sorrow when these bad men nailed Jesus to the cross. His heart broke as He watched Jesus go through all this pain and suffering, hanging on that cross. Jesus had never ever done anything to cause any harm in any way to any person! All He had ever done in all His life was to love people, heal people from their sicknesses, and try to show them how to live a good life. Even as Jesus died He was asking for the forgiveness of these men. He said they didn't fully understand what they were doing.

But something wonderful happened. After three days Jesus rose and came back to life again. No man could die and live again unless God gave them life. Jesus went to Heaven to prepare homes for every single person who asks for forgiveness so that one day they can live a peaceful life forever.

Grandma said that if a boy or girl or mom or dad ever did something wrong and were truly sorry for what they had done that they could always pray to God for forgiveness and say they never wanted to be bad like that again. And if they genuinely asked Him to, God would forgive everything they'd asked. It would be like He was throwing those sins to the bottom of the sea where no one else could see. These bad things would be remembered by God no more.

If anyone felt lonesome or sad because someone said things about them that weren't true they had one friend, Jesus, who would always understand and help them through the sad times.

Grandma told Mikey of the many times Jesus walked many, many miles to help someone and while he walked He had to leave His home far behind.

She told him of the verse that said that the foxes have their holes and the birds have their nests, but the Son of Man (Jesus) had no place to lay His head. His home and His bed were so far away as He tried to help others. Sometimes He'd be so far away from home and so tired from walking all day that He'd simply wrap his coat around Him and lay His head on some rock under some bushes. But that didn't stop Him from helping others.

"Well, it's time for us to go to bed. Tomorrow is another day," Grandpa yawned. After Mikey took his shower he and Grandma knelt to say their good-night prayers, as they always did every night. "Loving Father, thank you for such a beautiful day you gave us. Help us to always be loving and kind like the Boy Jesus was. Please take care of us tonight as we sleep and all our animals ('and especially

Hound Dog,' Mikey chimed in) in Jesus name we pray. Amen."

As Grandma tucked Mikey under his covers that night and gave him a big kiss it felt so good to have a bed of his own and to have people to love him.

Mikey had been so busy that day, as he usually was; he was so tired, and he just fell asleep without even listening to see if he heard the foxes bark any more. But Hound Dog was listening, you could count on that.

Best Buddies

Chapter 4

MORNING ON THE FARM

The next day Mikey was up to hear the rooster crowing. You see Grandma taught school to many boys and girls. She had several miles to drive before she got to school so she had to get up early and make a good breakfast for Grandpa and Mikey and pack her own lunch before she left.

"Bye, ya'll be good boys today," Grandma laughed, as she gave Mikey a hug and patted Hound Dog on the nose. "And you, too," she chuckled as she gave Grandpa a special kiss.

Grandpa, Mikey, and Hound Dog would first get on to their duties on this side of the creek.

Grandpa loved to hand-feed the cows and horses. He'd give Mikey an ear of corn to feed to them. At first Mikey was afraid the big animals would nibble his fingers but he soon learned how to be a miniature Grandpa and follow his example.

After Grandpa fed Daisy, the Jersey cow, he'd let her out the barn door and know exactly where she'd go. She'd slowly walk on up the gravel road to another pasture of Grandpa's, eating flowers and tender leaves on the way. Then she'd go into that pasture and spend the whole day by herself munching all the tender grasses and drinking cool water from the creek.

When she grew tired she'd lie down in the grass and chew her cud. The "cud" was a ball of grass she'd eaten during the day and then burped it back up into her mouth to chew it really good.

Mikey laughed at Daisy. She looked like she was chewing chewing gum!

"Did you know Daisy has four sections to her stomach?" Grandpa asked Mikey. "It's almost like she has four stomachs."

"Four stomachs! No wonder Daisy is such a big animal!" Mikey laughed.

As Daisy chewed her cud she'd look all around the peaceful pasture as she watched the birds flitting around and listened to their songs. Soon she'd nod her head as she caught a little nap. But when the sun started getting lower in the sky she'd usually come slowly walking back to the barn for Grandpa to hand-feed her some corn again. Once in a great while she seemed to be so busy munching away or drinking out of the cool creek that Grandpa, Mikey, and Hound Dog would go after her but most of the time she wandered up and down that road on her own.

One day Hound Dog was all alert! There was a new little baby beside Old Grace, the brown mare. He put on his brakes when he saw this new little creature and sniffed and sniffed the air to see what was going on.

He craned and craned his neck and finally touched the new baby with his little nose and yep, she smelled like she really belonged here and Grandpa was petting her so everything must be all right.

Soon the new baby could skim around the pasture so fast on those slender little legs that Cousin Benita named her Satellite like the big satellites that skim around the skies far overhead.

Satellite was so cute, brown with a white streak down her nose. She would kick up her heels and frolic around! Hound Dog had to keep away from those sharp heels. He didn't dare get too close. You never knew when Satellite could spin around fast in her play.

One day when Cousin Benita, Aunt Nita, and Uncle Roy came to visit the farm they were all walking in the pasture when they spied a persimmon tree. Yum-m! They loved persimmons. You had to get them after the frost came and made them nice and ripe. If you got one before the cold frost made them that ripe, whew! your mouth puckered up. They didn't taste good at all.

So everybody was picking up good ripe persimmons that had fallen under the tree and munching away. And of course Satellite had to come join the fun. Uncle Roy gave her a handful of persimmons as they walked along. Apparently a particular persimmon must have puckered her lips.

All of a sudden Satellite kicked up her back heels and Uncle Roy had to get out of the way right quick like. "Whew!" He said, all out of breath. "Boy! She almost got me that time. I could feel the hair on her hoof swishing right above my eyebrow! That was too close!"

That could have been a serious accident and everyone breathed a sigh of relief that Uncle Roy wasn't hurt. No more persimmons for Satellite! But after that, Satellite walked along with the rest of them as if to say, "Sorry 'bout that! Wow! That made you want to slap your pappy!" (That was an old saying these country people liked to say when they felt extra good, and mischievous.)

After they finished feeding Hound Dog, the cows, the horses, and chickens, Grandpa said, "Well, are you ready to go with me over to the cabin?" Grandpa already knew Mikey liked to go help him at the cabin— well, he maybe didn't always help, but he liked to at least be with Grandpa.

Grandpa and Mikey could be two big teases. Grandpa could laugh and tell you some of the funniest stories. Most of the stories were things he did when he was little.

Ever since Mikey was just a little boy, so little he couldn't even walk yet; he was just inside his little walker waddling around when he'd see something funny. He would just laugh and laugh and make everyone around him laugh, too! And he grew up like Grandpa making people laugh! They were fun to be around.

One day when Mikey was about four-years-old Aunt Nita took him shopping with her. They got to the counter where Aunt Nita was going to pay the lady for what she was buying. Mikey leaned on the counter. He was just tall enough that his big blue eyes could peep over the counter. As he looked up at the lady she smiled brightly, "Where did you get those big, blue eyes?" she laughingly asked.

"Oh, I've had these eyes for a l-o-n-g t-i-m-e," he answered. Aunt Nita and the lady couldn't help it—they laughed and laughed. It was so cute the way Mikey thought of that answer. And it was so cute the way his southern drawl stretched out "l-o-n-g t-i-m-e."

Then there was the day Aunt Nita was sitting outside giving her poodle a hair cut. After she trimmed his top-knot she looked around to see Mikey with a caterpillar stretched out on a finger. In the other hand he had his little scissors. The caterpillar had long hairs sticking up on its head. Mikey was trimming those hairs with his scissors. How on earth did Mikey find that caterpillar so fast and even think to trim the caterpillar's top-knot! What a quick little mind! For years Aunt Nita laughed about that one.

Another time Mikey was sitting with Grandma in church. He whispered, "Grandma, are my chicken feathers okay?"

Grandma looked at Mikey questioningly. Had he brought some

chicken feathers to church? Then Mikey stroked the top of his head to smooth down his "rooster tail." Grandma almost cackled out loud right there in church. When a little boy had hairs sticking out on top his head, near the back, they called it a "rooster tail." She guessed a "rooster tail" could also be "chicken feathers." What a funny Mikey. It was so much fun watching him grow up!

How on earth did Mikey find that caterpillar so fast and even think to trim the caterpillar's top-knot! What a quick little mind! For years Aunt Nita laughed about that one.

Grandpa built houses to sell. Right now he was fixing up an old log home just across the creek. This used to be the house of two older women. There were two big rooms. These two women liked to have their own rooms. Between the rooms was what they called a "breeze-way." Sure enough the breeze went through that "breeze-way" like it was a tunnel that drew in the breezes. People liked to sit in that breeze-way. It felt so cool, especially on a hot summer day.

Each room had its own fireplace made of big rocks. Well, Grandpa repaired the fireplaces and made them look like new. He combined the breeze-way and the two rooms together and made big bedrooms in what used to be the attic. By the time he got through with this house and carpeted it, it looked absolutely beautiful. He would sell it to a kind man and his wife who helped many young people to overcome some problems for which they needed special help.

One of the neat things about this land and this house was the swinging bridge one had to go over to get to the house on the other side of the creek.

At first, Mikey was afraid to go over this bridge. Every time he took a step the bridge would swing. He felt like he was going to fall. But before you knew it he had so much fun going over that bridge and wasn't afraid any more.

Hound Dog loved that bridge. He would go ahead of Mikey, his tail wagging, his feet padding until he got to the other side where he galloped down the steps. Yes, Mikey and Hound Dog had so much fun going over that bridge. Not every boy or girl had a bridge like this.

The people who bought the house that Grandpa built loved that bridge, too. In fact, they named the place, "The Bridge" because it was not only a bridge to get over the creek but because it was a bridge to help young people get things straight in their minds and then go back on the other side a new person.

Chapter 5

A COLD, ICY SURPRISE

One cold winter day when family friends came to visit Grandma and Grandpa, they all wanted to take a walk. They decided to go over the swinging bridge to the other side to see the newest things Grandpa had done to the cabin. As usual Hound Dog led the way. Remember, Hound Dog loved that bridge and was always taking little trips across it whether he was all alone or with a group of people.

On this day Hound Dog was loping across the bridge in high-style. He would show everyone else how to go. When Hound Dog was just about across the bridge, suddenly the bridge made a big squeaking sound! Then, crash! A big, strong cable broke! One side of the bridge swung down, dumping everyone into the icy cold water. Whew! That was the furthest thing anyone was thinking about. Suddenly all the excited talk everyone had been doing, expressing how Hound Dog was strutting etc., etc., erupted into yells and screams.

Mikey was riding on an uncle's shoulders. The uncle had his hands in his pockets while Mikey had his arms around Uncle's head, but as they hit the water, Mikey hadn't fallen off. He still had his arms around Uncle's head and Uncle still had his hands in his pockets! But that didn't last for long. Mikey started screaming and scrambling as fast as he could go over the slippery rocks to get to the roots of the trees on the other side of the creek. Nobody knew that Mikey could move so fast!

Ooh-h-h! That water was soooo cold! Everybody was yelling all at once when the cold water soaked their clothes and splashed on their faces! That was an experience that no one of them would ever forget.

But they were all so thankful that no one got hurt!

As they all fell all those feet into the water, they looked up to see that Hound Dog was the only one to make it to the other side of the bridge without falling off. When he felt the commotion beneath him, he ran as fast he could, his tail flying. He didn't stop to look back. His eyes looked only one way. He was getting off that bridge and right quick like. But once he got off that bridge he ran back and forth in circles to see what was happening to everyone else.

Grandpa went back to see what went wrong. Why did that strong cable break? Much to his dismay he saw something he hadn't noticed before. Some dirt had gotten piled up on a tree just where the strong cable was attached to the tree. That dirt had caused rust to form on the cable. The rust had eaten through the cable that caused the strong cable to become weak—weak enough to cause a bridge to collapse and dump all those people in the water. Someone could have been hurt badly all because of a little rust.

Later, Grandpa stretched a whole new strong cable to the tree and the little swinging bridge was all new again. But never, ever again, no matter how much they begged, Hound Dog would never go over that bridge again. He must have thought that bridge had betrayed him.

Grandpa told Mikey so many times it's the little things that eventually make big things come tumbling down. He once heard of a big city clock that kept such good time that all the people could always count on. Then one day the clock kept losing time and then finally the big clock stopped completely. When someone went up to see what was wrong with the big clock he was so surprised to find that it was only one little spider. Apparently the little spider had been working so hard that he made his web strong enough to clog up the clock's moving parts.

Among all the many things that Grandpa could do, he was an electrician. He could work on electrical problems and make them all okay again. You know what it's like to have the electricity go off. You can't cook. You can't turn on the lights. You can't turn on the heat in the winter time nor the air conditioner in the summer time. It's just usually a miserable time when the electricity goes off. Well, one time someone called Grandpa to help—"Help our electricity has gone off!"

Grandpa found that the problem was only a bobby pin that had fallen off in back of a refrigerator, hanging over some wires that made the connection go wrong. Everyone was so surprised that such a little thing could make all the electricity go off.

Ever since Grandpa had been a little boy he'd been told that it was the little foxes that spoiled the vines. It was the little animals that often played among the grapevines or even ate the grapes or berries from vines and left them all in a mess. Like the little rust that grew on the strong cable, Grandpa learned many years before how to be careful of the little problems before they grew to be big problems.

Chapter 6

MIKEY AND HOUND DOG IN
BIG TROUBLE

Sometimes Grandpa would be so busy with his work on the house that he lost all track of time and Hound Dog and Mikey would go over to the other side of the creek where Grandpa's house and barn were. Grandpa always felt good that Hound Dog would be taking care of Mikey.

Hound Dog would do some funny things that made Mikey laugh his head off. Hound Dog would see a big bird like a hawk or a vulture flying overhead in a circle and he'd go running in a circle underneath the bird, barking loudly. He seemed to think he could catch that big bird. But the funniest thing of all was when an airplane flew overhead. Hound Dog seemed to think it was just another big bird, the biggest bird he'd seen, and he'd run under the airplane trying to catch the big bird, or he'd even try to catch the airplane's shadow.

Mikey laughed and laughed as he watched Hound Dog's antics but all the laughing in the world didn't bother Hound Dog. He was on his mission to take care of Grandpa's farm. Hound Dog would literally run himself ragged trying to catch the bird. Poor Hound Dog! He wouldn't know what to do if he ever caught that big bird!

About mid-morning Mikey and Hound Dog would go for their Easter Egg Hunt. Mikey would get a special basket Grandma had given him to put the eggs in that he'd gather.

The big chickens liked to lay their eggs in the barn in special nest boxes made for them but those little Banti hens, they were out as usual choosing new nests. But all the hens just couldn't help it. When they'd lay an egg they would cackle big and loud to let everybody know they'd laid an egg. They seemed to be so proud of what they'd done. So Mikey would listen for the little Banti hens to cackle. They'd told on themselves. They'd told Mikey and Hound Dog exactly where their nest was. Then Mikey and Hound Dog went right to the nest and gathered each egg. But the hens wanted to lay lots of eggs in a nest so all those eggs would hatch baby chicks. They didn't want Mikey to take their eggs.

Mikey was always glad to see Grandma come home from school. One day when she came home from school she saw Mikey up in an apple tree. It wasn't anything new to see Mikey up in a tree. He loved to climb trees. But it was a surprise when she saw why Mikey was up in that tree today.

Mikey had followed a big long snake up that tree. He loved to play with snakes. Grandma and Grandpa had tried to teach Mikey the differences between the good snakes and the bad snakes. There weren't many bad snakes (the poison snakes) on their farm. Mainly there was just one kind of poisonous snake anywhere around their farm. It was a copperhead snake. In fact, there were just four kinds of poisonous snakes in the whole United States of America:

1) The rattlesnake. It has a rattle on the end of its tail. It will almost always rattle when you come near.

2) The copperhead, it is spotted with a head that looks like it has copper on it.

3) The water moccasin or cottonmouth, is usually a big, fat snake. It's soft spots sort of run together making it look more black than spotted. Sometimes when it lays on a rock, sunning, it opens its mouth which is all white inside like it has cotton in its mouth. Often when it sees danger

it will open it's mouth and you can see it is white.

4) The coral snake. It is a beautiful snake with a black snout then a yellow band around it, then a red band, a yellow band, then a black band. The yellow and red bands are next to each other. There are other beautiful snakes with red snouts, but the red and yellow bands are separated. They aren't poisonous snakes.

Three types of poisonous snakes in the USA have fangs. The fangs are like tubes inside its mouth full of poison. These three types of snakes have fat, triangular heads. The coral snake is different. It doesn't have fangs. It's head looks more pointed and is black. Its red bands are next to its yellow bands.

Anyhow, Grandma and Grandpa thought they had taught Mikey well about leaving snakes alone until you really know if its a good snake or a bad snake. But this particular day when Grandma saw Mikey up the tree holding this big snake, she gasped, "Mikey, how do you know this isn't a poison snake!"

"Oh, I opened its mouth and saw that it didn't have fangs!"

Grandma almost fainted! "Oh, no! You don't ever open a snake's mouth to see if it has fangs!" she protested. That would be too late. It would most likely have already bitten you before you got that close!"

When Grandma told Grandpa about this they both couldn't believe it! They never dreamed Mikey thought he should open a snake's mouth! Wow!

They had told Mikey about his guardian angel that watched over him all day long and that if ever he were in trouble he could always ask God to help him. But they realized more than ever how much that guardian angel means to every boy and girl to grow up in one piece!

Yes, Siree! Mikey was one of a kind! You just didn't know what he could come up with. He was the kind of boy that could reach into the hay and come out with a handful of tiny, pink, baby mice! He could just go up to a fly and catch it while Grandpa tried his best to even swat a fly. It seemed like that fly knew what the fly swatter meant.

Mikey loved to catch shiny green June bugs. He'd watch the big fat hens chase the June bugs. They usually flew close to the ground.

"Grandma, please tie a string on this June bug's leg for me," Mikey pleaded. Grandma remembered when she was a little girl and did the same thing. Mikey let the June bug go and it would fly to the end of its string and buzz and buzz. Mikey would make it go around in a circle. After awhile Mikey asked Grandma to help him untie the June bug and then he would let it fly away.

Sometimes Mikey would catch a big horse fly, hold onto the tippy end of its body and watch it buzz and buzz. Then he'd let it go.

Mikey loved to catch a baby lizard, tie a string around it's neck (not tight enough that it would hurt the lizard) and tie the other end of the string around a button on his shirt then let the little lizard crawl up his chest. When it started to crawl on his neck he couldn't take it, he got so tickled and carefully put it back down on his arm.

Mikey had fun watching all the little critters. He liked playing with the grand-daddy-longlegs.

Sometimes he'd pitch a grand-daddy-longlegs on Hound Dog and laugh and laugh as Hound Dog shook it off. When you heard Mikey laugh with that kind of laugh and you knew

Hound Dog was around you'd always have to check and see what Mikey was up to now. He loved to tease!

Speaking of grand-daddy-long-legs, Mikey loved to go with Hound Dog down to the creek and wade around. He liked catching crawdads. He always made sure he didn't catch them where they could turn around and clamp onto his fingers with their claws. That was another fun thing for Mikey. He liked to tease Hound Dog by putting a crawdad up to Hound Dog's whiskers and try to get the crawdad to hang onto a whisker and then laugh his head off watching Hound Dog try to get the crawdad off.

One day when Mikey and Hound Dog came home from a walk in the woods Mikey's eyes were as big as saucers as he told Grandpa he'd seen a monkey out in the woods. "Now, Mikey, you know there are no monkeys around here."

When Grandpa laughing told Grandma about Mikey finding a monkey in the woods they both laughed. But then, Grandma, said, "Well, you know Mikey finds so many things we never even thought about. Who knows, maybe somebody's pet monkey did get loose. Maybe he did see a monkey after all!" Or was it just an opossum hanging by it's tail onto a branch high in a tree? Most likely they'd never know but they'd have to listen to Mikey's tales and take them all very seriously!

Mikey would chase a rabbit through the woods and try to catch it. He and Hound Dog would end up going in circles trying to catch that rabbit.

Or Mikey would hear a bird scolding him and know that there was a nest nearby or Mama wouldn't be so upset. He'd try to get ever and ever closer to try to find the nest and peek inside to see the eggs or the baby birds.

One particular day, Mikey and Hound Dog saw so many things they wanted to investigate. They just kept wandering and wandering after this rabbit, that bird, tried to catch that frog.

They'd go around that briar patch, climb that big rock, ride those saplings down, swing on that grapevine, get a drink out of that spring—oh, they were having so much fun! They walked and walked, investigating that hole in the tree, trying to catch that pretty butterfly.

Soon they were tired and their stomachs started growling. They thought of those good sandwiches Grandma had made for them and those Little Debbie® cakes.

"We'd better go back home," Mikey said. He looked around him and all he saw was trees and more trees. It dawned on him that he really didn't know where home was. He didn't know which way to even start to go home. Hound Dog was just nosing around wherever Mikey went. It didn't matter to him which way was home. He didn't even know Mikey had decided to go home. He was just there for the adventure. Wherever Mikey went, he went.

Up on a wooded hillside Mikey saw three or four goats nimbly walking along a rocky ledge. They caught sight of Mikey about the same time he saw them. They stood still, carefully watching Hound Dog. They knew these rocks and these hills, every single inch of them.

Once these goats had lived on a farm inside a fence; like Hound Dog they didn't like to be cooped up in a pen. They wanted to be free so one day they got through the fence and nibbled from this bush and that bush, and drank out of this spring and that spring, going further and further from home until they didn't really know where home was anymore.

Sometimes their stomachs would be so hungry for the sweet food that Farmer Jones always gave them and wish they had never left the farm but when they tried to go anywhere near a farm the dogs would chase them away. Dogs could easily kill goats. All they had to do was run after the goats and the goats would soon get so out of breath that they would die.

So these goats had learned to stay far away from the dogs. The pads on their hooves seemed to stick to the rock ledges like glue. They knew where to go that was hard for dogs to go. Now when people caught a glimpse of these goats they called them, "wild goats."

Mikey watched the goats high on the ledges and wondered if he would be a "wild boy" never finding his way home. He sat down and listened and listened to hear all he could hear. Far, far away he heard some cows mooing.

"Let's go find the cows!" Mikey called to Hound Dog. They walked and walked and kept walking toward the sound of the cows. Finally, they came out of the woods and into a pasture. The cows hadn't seen them yet. They were glad to see the cows but uh-oh! Mikey saw something that really scared him! In the middle of the herd of cows was the big monster of a bull.

"Oh, no! We've got to get over the fence before the big bull sees us!" Mikey thought to himself. Hound dog was staying close to Mikey, just sniffing the air. Mikey didn't dare call Hound Dog. He just hoped the bull wouldn't see Hound Dog.

Some cows on the outside of the herd started to lower their heads and stare as they now saw the movement of Hound Dog.

"Oh, no! Hound Dog, stay close to me." "We've got to go as quietly as we can to the corner of this pasture and through that fence."

As Mikey started to hurry toward the fence corner, the cows were coming closer to see what was going on. He couldn't let that bull see him! He didn't care if he ran through cow pies or not, he must get out of here before the big bull saw them.

Finally, he reached the fence and rolled under the barbed wires and began to call for Hound Dog to follow. As he held the fence up for Hound Dog he heard the bull start to bellow. He saw his big sides heaving as he ran toward them. But it was too late for the bull to reach them but just in time for Mikey and Hound Dog to find safety.

Mikey was so out of breath. That was a real scare for him. He never, ever wanted to go through something like that again. He patted Hound Dog on the head, "Thank you! Thank you! Hound Dog for not causing a ruckus back there with that bull," Hound Dog gave him a little nudge as if to say, "Silly, I know how to take care of myself around a bull. I know when to bark and when not to bark. You just don't know all the times I've been around different dangerous animals when you're sound asleep at night!"

As Mikey looked all around him he could see a road. "Come on, let's get to the road. Maybe someone will come along and help us to get home, Hound Dog!" Hound Dog knew what a road was for sure. That's what all dogs know. They like to walk the roads and know just which way to go.

They walked and walked along this winding road. Mikey was getting more and more hungry, He wished so badly that someone would come along. Finally, off in the distance he heard a car.

"Stay with me, Hound Dog! Here comes a car. Maybe we can catch a ride."

The car started to go past them. Mikey felt so let-down! But the wife said, "What is that little boy doing all by himself on a road way out here? He must be lost."

The man slowed down and backed up the car. "Where are you headed?" asked the kind man.

"We got lost, Hound Dog and me! We don't know where we are but we want to go home."

"Hop in! Let's see if we can find your home."

Mikey tried and tried to get Hound Dog to get in the car but Hound Dog would have nothing to do with it. He remembered that's the way he lost his mama and his doggie family. He also knew when he got into the truck that Grandpa took him to the vet where he got a shot and he didn't like that vet and what he did to him. No Siree. Hound Dog was not going to get in that car. He slunk back into the bushes beside the road and trotted off.

"I don't want to go without Hound Dog," Mikey had big tears in his eyes. "Oh, don't worry about him," the kind man said. "He looks like a smart dog and he'll find his way home just fine."

Before you knew it they went up the hill and around the curve and there it was! "Oh, there's the church where I go! I know exactly how to get home now!" He told the man to turn up the hill to the left. Then in a few minutes he told him to go to that road on the left and it would go right by Grandpa's house. The man and his wife were so very glad to be able to help this little boy find his way home.

When they pulled up to Grandpa's house Grandpa came running out. He'd been so busy pounding away with his hammer that he simply didn't realize so much time had gone by since he'd seen Mikey and Hound Dog. He thought they were just over on the other side of the creek hunting Easter eggs! And then Grandpa got hungry and realized it was time to eat.

Usually when it was lunchtime it was Mikey he heard saying, "Grandpa, I'm hungry, can we go home to eat!" So Grandpa was surprised when his stomach started to growl and he hadn't heard that little voice from Mikey saying he was hungry.

Grandpa looked around him but there was no Mikey and no Hound Dog! He called and called for them and thought, "They must be over hunting eggs." So, he went across the bridge thinking surely he'd find them on the other side by the house and barn.

When Grandpa got to the house Mikey and Hound Dog were no where to be found. He called and called and couldn't find them. He was really getting worried! He was just about to get in the truck and go up and down the road calling Mikey and Hound Dog's name.

When he saw Mikey's little round face peering out the window of that car he was overjoyed but he wondered why Mikey was in that car!

Mikey jumped out of the car and into Grandpa's arms. "Oh, Grandpa. We got lost in the woods. We didn't know where we were. I was afraid I might not ever find home again!" And the big tears started to fall and he hugged Grandpa tightly!

When the man explained how he'd seen Mikey and Hound Dog walking along the road so far away, Grandpa couldn't believe they'd been that many miles away.

Mikey had lots of things to tell Grandpa to fill in the rest of the story. But Grandpa kept telling the man how thankful he was for bringing Mikey home. The man just smiled and said how glad he was to find Mikey and how glad he was that Mikey knew just how to get home. "Well, it's nice meeting you," he told Grandpa, "but we'd better get on our way to our appointment."

When the car left, Grandpa couldn't help it. He was so choked up that he hugged Mikey tightly but he also just couldn't help it. He scolded Mikey for wandering off. At the same time he blamed himself for letting so much time go by without checking to see if Mikey was okay.

Mikey knew he deserved for Grandpa to be mad at him. He also knew that he would never ever let himself get lost in the woods again! It was too scary to think you might not ever find home again.

He told Grandpa all about the big bull, too! And now he said he was worried that Hound Dog would be lost. "I tried and tried to get Hound

81

Dog in the car but he just wouldn't get in the car. Oh, no, I'm afraid he won't come back and it will be all my fault!" Now Mikey really began to cry.

"Oh, Hound Dog will come back home. He knows where home is. He can follow his own tracks back home. Don't you worry about Hound Dog! I just want you to promise me you'll never ever wander off like that again!"

"Oh, no, Grandpa. I was really scared. I won't ever do that again!"

"Well, let's just thank God for sending your guardian angel to take care of you each day and especially for taking care of you today and helping just the right person to come along to bring you home safely! All kinds of bad things could have happened but they didn't, and now you're safe at home again!"

"Grandpa, I'm so tired and hungry. Can we eat!""

"Yes, Sir, I'm so hungry, too. Let's go eat those good sandwiches Grandma made for us and a Little Debbie®, too!"

Never did those sandwiches taste so good as they did that day when Mikey was safe at home again.

By the time Grandma got home from school, there was Hound Dog! His tongue was hanging out. He had scratches all over him but he ran up and started giving Mikey big slurpy kisses all over his face! Mikey's big tears spilled over into Hound Dog's face and he hugged him for all he was worth.

"I'm so sorry, Hound Dog! It's all my fault that we got lost! I'm so glad you're back home!" He gave Hound Dog one of his sandwiches. Hound Dog gobbled down the sandwich but he was just too tired to do another thing. He flopped down in a sunny spot and fell fast asleep but his legs were still jerking. He was having dreams of losing his way home and having a hard time getting past that old bull! He was too tired to even chase the big birds in the sky. Let them be! He was going to take a snooze!

You better believe it! That night Mikey almost went to sleep while he was having his prayer but he had so much to be thankful for that day! No sooner had Grandma tucked him in bed than Mikey was sound asleep. Tomorrow would be another day but not a day like today!

Chapter 7

BOB'S BONFIRE

The next day Mikey and Hound Dog stayed close to Grandpa as he hammered all those nails, making the cabin beautiful. But Mikey was still so young. He had much to learn in days to come.

Mikey loved the bonfire Grandpa made for him and his cousins. "Grandpa, when are you going to make another bonfire! Can we have one soon?"

"Well, it would be fun to have a bonfire again. I'll talk with Grandma and see if we can have one. The nights are getting pretty cool and it would be great to have a bonfire!"

But making that bonfire and the interest that Mikey had in the bonfire made Grandpa remember about another little boy about Mikey's age. He decided now would be a good time to tell Mikey a story:

One day a little boy, we'll call him Bob, just couldn't keep his mind off those matches. He wanted to make a bonfire just like his dad made. He knew that Dad gathered some dry sticks and piled those sticks in a big tent-shape. Then Dad struck a match to make the big bonfire.

So, Bob would prove that he could make a big bonfire, too. Today he'd just practice, but another day he would make a bonfire for his friends to enjoy!

Bob scurried around to find some dry sticks to make a tent for the bonfire. After he made the tent, he tried to light the match. But he had a book of these paper matches and every time he'd try to light a match it would finally make a little flame but the match would bend and the little flame would go out.

Finally, one of the matches lit. But Bob wasn't so happy when the flame almost burned his finger before he could let it go.

"Ouch!" Bob yelled! He quickly threw the match on the dry sticks and wow! It did start a fire! He felt like he finally did something right. But the little flame lit another stick and another stick and lit the dry grass all around the tent and licked the dry leaves up all around it.

As the roar of the fire spread, getting bigger and bigger, Bob's big dog, Rambo, began to get excited. He barked loudly. Something was wrong, Rambo knew! "Dad, come see what Bob has done," he seemed to yell.

Dad heard Rambo barking and he knew what that bark meant—something was wrong. He smelled the fire and saw it getting bigger. He ran to get the garden hose and sprayed water all over the fire. His eyes stung! It was getting harder to breathe from all the smoke!

It was windy enough that day that the fire was just going too fast. Luckily Mom heard all the commotion and smelled all the smoke and quickly filled up a bucket and ran to throw bucket after bucket on the fire.

Bob was so afraid. He ran to hide in the bushes far away from the fire.

"What on earth were you trying to do?" Mom and Dad both scolded when they spied Bob trying to hide.

Bob was shivering with fright. He had no idea such a big fire would come so fast from that little match. He starting crying, "I was just trying to see if I could make a bonfire like Dad does," he sobbed. "I won't ever do it again."

"That little match could burn our whole house down, our barn, all our chickens and animals. You must never ever light a match unless you let

Dad or Mom help you, do you understand." They had to be sure Bob understood what danger they could all be in from a fire.

Bob knew full well that he deserved to be scolded. But he already knew he would never do this again. Then Mom and Dad hugged him close to their hearts. They wanted him to know how very much they loved him and how much they forgave him for causing such a big problem that could have even gotten bigger than anyone could expect. They, too, remembered days when they were growing up and learned some big lessons.

Grandpa told Mikey of some pretty stupid things he had done when he was growing up from which he learned lessons. He wanted Mikey to know that every little boy and girl can learn things from their moms and dads, grandmas and grandpas, aunts and uncles, and teachers, of how not to get into trouble.

The kids when Grandpa was growing up would often dare him to do things. And sometimes Grandpa would want to act big and do some things they dared him to do.

Grandpa remembered one day the boys dared each other to crack an egg into their open mouths and swallow the raw egg. Ugh! That didn't sound good at all to Grandpa but he wanted to be big like the rest of them. He didn't want them to make fun of him because he wouldn't do it, so Grandpa broke the egg into his mouth but the yellow yolk got stuck in his mouth.

Granda couldn't get that egg yolk up nor get it down! His eyes started bugging out. His face was getting red. He just couldn't swallow that egg yolk. Finally, he felt like he was going to vomit and up came the egg yolk splattering all over his shirt.

The boys just laughed and laughed at Grandpa Norman. But he decided that to act big he had to BE big. From now on he wouldn't let any other kid trick him into taking a silly dare just to act big.

The next time, the boys dared him to swallow a gold fish that was swimming around in its bowl. They picked it up and ordered him to open his mouth and swallow it. But Grandpa Norman walked away and said if they wanted to swallow a gold fish that was their choice but he wasn't going to swallow any gold fish. That was just plain stupid! The boys finally decided they couldn't make Grandpa Norman do what they ordered him to do or dared him to do.

Grandpa knew that all those you thought were true friends wouldn't always be what you thought they were. Sometimes even those you thought you could trust the very most, you really couldn't trust. You had to use your own head, your own brain to think things through that you knew were right or wrong. God always helped you to know what was right. You just had to be strong enough to do what was right no matter what someone else thought of you. And each day you would ask God to give you the strength you needed for that day.

Grandma gave Mikey a toothpick. She asked him if he could break that toothpick. Of course he could break that toothpick. That was easy. Then Grandma got a nail and put the toothpick right next to the nail. Now she asked Mikey if he could break the toothpick and the nail together. No, now Mikey couldn't break that tooth-pick. It had the strong nail beside it. She told Mikey that God was just like that nail. Anytime we ask God to be with us He will always give us the strength we can't have if we stand alone by ourselves.

Grandma told Mikey of when she was a little girl. She had three big brothers and four sisters. Wow! Mikey thought that was a big family. Grandma Ruth trusted her brothers and sisters but she learned that sometimes you can't even trust people in your own family. You have to do what you know is the right thing to do regardless of what anyone on earth says.

Grandma Ruth's mom and dad were farmers and they didn't have much money for their big family so the kids didn't get many toys. Their mom and dad would often make them neat little toys. But one day Mama gave Ruth a little doll. It was the only doll Ruth ever had had. It was a tiny rubber doll that had a squeaker in it. When you squeezed the doll it would squeak.

Oh, how Ruth loved her baby doll. She named her Baby Betty and took Baby Betty with her everywhere she would go.

One day Ruth was standing by her big brother Wilbur, watching him draw up water from the well. The well was a deep well. It wasn't any bigger around than a saucer. If you squinted your eyes and looked down, far down into that deep, dark well, and the sun was shining just right you might see just a little tiny glimpse of water flickering way way down in that well, a glimmer of water flickering in the sunlight.

There was a long tube of a bucket tied good and tight to a rope. You could let that long bucket down in the well and hear it far below hit the water, then let it sink into the water and hear it fill up, then you could draw up a bucket of water.

This day Grandma Ruth's big brother, Wilbur, had an idea. "Ruth pitch Baby Betty down in the well and I will bring her up again!"

Oh, my! Ruth didn't dare throw Baby Betty down in that well. "Oh, no," she cried, "not Baby Betty."

"Oh, come on, scaredy cat. I'll bring her back up. Don't you trust me? If you really trust me you'll throw her down the well."

Ruth looked into brother Wilbur's eyes. She really did trust Wilbur. She wanted him to know that she loved and trusted him. So, she quickly, before she could think about it any more, threw Baby Betty down the well.

You could hear Baby Betty squeaking all the way down as she hit the sides of the dark well. Every squeak Ruth could hear sounded like Baby Betty crying for her mama Ruth. Ruth's heart was about to break. She didn't want Baby Betty to think she would throw her down that dark well!

"Hurry and bring Baby Betty back up to me," she cried to Brother Wilbur.

Brother Wilbur let the bucket down, down in the well. It hit the water; he waited for it to fill and then brought the bucket up again.

Ruth expected to see Baby Betty but there was no Baby Betty. The tears filled Ruth's eyes. Wilbur tried and tried to get Baby Betty back up but Ruth never saw Baby Betty again.

Ruth ran home and sobbed and sobbed for Baby Betty. Her heart was broken. Her mom felt so terrible about the loss of Baby Betty to her little girl's heart. She scolded Wilbur soundly. She tried to get him to see what he had done to a little girl's trust in him. But she tried her best to get Ruth to see that she should always do what she knew was right and not just do what anyone else would tell you to do no matter how you loved and thought you trusted that person.

Grandma knew that there would be times as Mikey grew up when his "friends" would try to get him to do things that he knew were wrong. Some would try to get him to try a little cigarette, "It won't hurt you just to try one," they'd say.

Or they'd say, "Just take a sip of this beer or whiskey! Oh, it won't hurt you just to try a little! Come, on, don't be a baby. You're man enough to know how much you can drink."

But Grandma and Grandpa knew that that was the way everyone got hooked into smoking and drinking, just to "try a little." The "little" didn't seem all that bad so they smoked more and drank more until they really didn't see anything wrong with it. Soon the "little" became BIG just like that "little" flame became a BIG fire! Oh, how they wanted Mikey to live a good, long life full of happiness.

"Tell you what! You can help me make a big bonfire next Saturday night when your cousins come up and we'll have a good time and a hayride afterwards," Grandpa said.

It had been another long, hard day but a day that Mikey would never forget. He loved his grandpa and grandma and knew that they loved him. He went to sleep that night looking at the bright moon peeping in his window and was so thankful he had a bed to sleep in that night and that all was well with the whole farm!

Chapter 8

GRANDPA NORMAN'S SPECIAL BONFIRE

Mikey could hardly wait until Saturday night would come and they could make that big bonfire and have that hayride! But finally, the big night came!

Mikey loved his cousins like they were his brothers and sisters. He always loved it when they came to visit. And they loved him like a little brother.

Grandma and Grandpa decided Grandpa's big trailer for the hayride would need more kids than just Mikey and his cousins and their families; so, they invited all their church to come and bring the kids for a fun night! They were invited to come in the afternoon and take a hike with them which everyone seemed to love to do.

Grandpa's farm was really different than the farms that were around. It was strange but there were Peruvian Daffodils, big, beautiful white flowers with long petals that spread out like a huge lily. They were on stalks about three feet high from the ground.

Grandma had lived near here all her life. Grandma loved all the plants. When she was little if she didn't know what a plant was she'd look it up in a book and remember its name. She had never seen the Peruvian Daffodil anywhere else except on this farm. She wondered how this plant got way up in Kentucky.

Uncle Roy said, "If it grows, Grandma knows!" It was amazing to him that anyone would know so many things in nature and remember their names! Uncle Roy, too, was one of those special people who remember so many details. He had grown up mainly in a big city but since he'd been living in the country he loved it so much. He felt so free. It was so peaceful!

Ever since Uncle Roy had been big enough to hold a fishing pole in his hand he'd loved to fish. Now when he went on fishing tournaments he'd say to his partner, "Hear that wren! See that green heron!" Uncle Roy wasn't a city boy anymore—he was a country boy and even surprised his country girl wife, Aunt Nita, by all the things he learned so quickly about country life.

Also, there were prickly pear cactus plants on their farm. Grandma never saw these cactus plants on any of the other farms around them unless someone had bought one and planted it by their house.

Grandma had explained to Mikey that when you see a plant that has three leaves growing on a vine or a bush, beware! When you walk on it or brush by it you probably will crush the leaves and its juice spreads on you. That juice is poison. Many people are highly allergic to that poison. Soon a red rash will appear on their skin. Then that rash usually turns into big blisters. The rash and blisters are very, very itchy.

It seemed like Aunt Nita could almost look at poison ivy or poison oak and get splashed with it's juice. When you got the rash and the big blisters like she did, it felt like many, many tiny gnats biting you all at once. You felt like you were going crazy with all that itching.

But Aunt Nita learned that just as soon as she got home she needed to thoroughly wash her face, her hands, her arms, and any skin that was showing, with a strong soap to try to wash all the poison juice off. She made sure she didn't go walking in the woods with shorts, but would wear long slacks or jeans and tall hiking boots.

**Poison Ivy Vine
(pointed lobes)**

**Poison Oak
(round lobes)**

**Beautiful
Peruvian
Daffodil**

For most people, when you first see the rash the doctor can give you a shot to stop the poison in its tracks.

Unfortunately, for Aunt Nita the shot never worked. The doctor tried freezing the splotches, giving her preventive drops, all kinds of things, but nothing worked. Her eyes would get so swollen that she could hardly see and she'd get huge blisters between her fingers. But she just had to endure it. Being a country girl she loved the woods even though she might end up with poison ivy or poison oak. But she tried her best to watch out for those three leaves, wear clothing over as much skin as possible and wash thoroughly after she got home

One tall, rocky, hill stood out near their house. They called it the pinnacle. Everybody wanted to climb to the top of the pinnacle. When they got to the top they could see all the pastures and woods from far around. But Grandma was the first to do something before the others even thought about it.

There were a few trees on top the pinnacle and after Grandma got to the top she climbed way up in one of those trees. Yep, Grandma was a special, special lady. She always had fun at whatever she did. The kids at school had fun learning with Grandma Ruth as their teacher. Grandpa had to work hard to keep up with Grandma Ruth!

There were tall rocky cliffs like the Rocky Mountains out West. Then there were big bluffs. Under one particular big bluff down by the creek they found many rocks that the Indians who lived in these hills many many years ago had made into corn grinders. They would find a bowl-like hollow in a rock, put their corn in the bowl and grind the corn with these corn grinders they had made.

There must have been a big tribe of Indians living by this creek. All along the banks of the creek when farmers would later plow up the ground for a cornfield their plows broke up lots of arrowheads. It was so much fun to see how many arrowheads you could find.

No wonder the Indians chose this place. They had all the water they needed from the many springs all around. They had lots of nuts from the trees around—hickory nuts, black walnuts, hazelnuts. There were lots and lots of huckleberry bushes, wild blueberries, and wild strawberries.

Grandma taught Mikey that some red berries were poisonous. So, don't eat every berry that's red thinking it is a wild strawberry. Never eat a white berry or any kind of mushroom out in the fields or woods without first asking an adult if its okay to eat it.

The cornfields Grandpa planted down by the creek made lots of corn. These Indians probably used these same fields for their corn. It was fun trying to imagine the Indian kids walking these same trails.

Long ago there was a robber named Jesse James. Everybody had heard of Jesse James. What he did robbing the people on stagecoaches, etc., was very bad but he was a very smart person. He knew how to hide so he wouldn't get caught. Well, the stories went that Jesse James came down what was now Grandpa's creek, riding on a raft, and that he hid in some of the caves that were around Grandpa's creek.

Stories were told about another family that traveled down this creek to try to make a home along its banks. There had been a lot of rain and the creek was flooded. The family had stacked lots of their belongings onto the flatbed boat they had made. All of a sudden the muddy, churned up creek waters made a sharp turn and the keg of molasses spilled out. For some reason the old timers seemed to remember the day the molasses ran down the river.

If you were to visit that creek today you could walk for miles and miles along beside it and never see any other farms. It looks like one huge woods that no one has ever been in before. If you see a fallen log, it's not because someone cut it down. It just grew old, got hollow and fell down.

Grandpa told Mikey, "See this big tree. It looks big and strong, doesn't it? But look, you can see on this side that there's a big hollow place. This big tree will fall soon because it has a bad heart. Sometimes you can see someone who really looks good but you have to try to see their heart if they are really a good person or are just pretending to be a good person. You have to listen to your friends' words and look at their actions to see if you really want to be good buddies with this boy or girl."

As everybody went on their walk this day they came to some big cliffs. Grandma saw some pretty dried flowers hanging over a big cliff. To this day Uncle Roy well remembers seeing Grandma so near the edge of that cliff. He gasped, and was so relieved when Grandma got away from that cliff.

Grandma was like one of those wild goats; she seemed to have feet like glue that stuck to the rocks but even grandmas need their guardian angels to watch over them, especially if you had a grandma like Grandma Ruth!

When they got back to Grandpa's house they were pretty tired out and just sat back and relaxed, sipping a big glass of Grandma's lemonade.

As they waited for it to get dark somebody started playing the piano and they all sang some songs. Grandpa asked each one of them what their favorite Bible verse was. Aunt Nita had always remembered that verse, ever since she'd been a little girl, about the foxes having their holes, and the birds having their nests but the Son of Man didn't have a place to lay His head.

Grandma remembered when she was a little girl she was so afraid of storms. When a big storm would come up, the rain would fall hard, the thunder would roll and the lightning flash and she'd always think of the verse that said that the angel of the Lord will stand by you and deliver you. Grandpa thanked the Lord for the beautiful day they had enjoyed and for the protection God had given and asked God to be with them tonight on their hayride.

Whoopee! Mikey could hardly wait until they lit the bonfire. The night was getting cool and the hot fire felt so good.

The day before, Grandpa had cut off some green sticks from living bushes. He'd made a green stick for each person to use to roast their marshmallows.

The dead, dry sticks wouldn't work. They'd burn too easily. You wouldn't want to roast a marshmallow on a stick that was just going to burn up in the fire. Grandpa was smarter than that.

Smores

Graham Cracker

Toasted Marshmallows

Hershey Chocolate Bar

Graham Cracker

Toasted Marshmallows

Canned Biscuit Dough

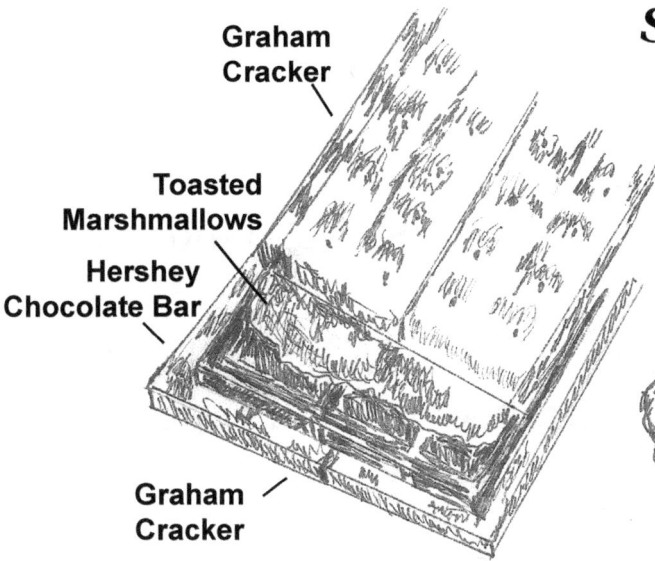

Fill toasted cup with jelly, and/or peanut butter.

BISCUITS

Wrap biscuit dough around green stick to form a cup. Toast.

Toasted Biscuit Cups

Grandpa let the bonfire burn down a little bit until there were just nice, red, glowing coals. Now you could roast your marshmallows without having your face and hands get toasted.

Grandpa let people pick out the stick they wanted from the pile of sticks he'd made. Mikey picked a stick that had several little branches on the end of it so that he could put several marshmallows on at one time to roast. Aunt Nita liked to toast a marshmallow, and then when it got nicely browned she'd pull off the brown part, eat it, and put the marshmallow over the coals again to toast the part that was left.

But wait, Grandma had thought of something else that was so yummy, as well! She'd brought out some Graham crackers and Hershey bars. You'd put a part of the Hershey bar on the Graham cracker, then put a toasted marshmallow or two on the

Hershey bar and squish them to-gether with another Hershey bar and Graham cracker on top You called those treats Smores. There couldn't be a better treat! That was absolutely scrumptious!

Grandma had made some hot chocolate to drink. It felt so good and warm going down your cold throat. It warmed you up all inside! Grand-ma was good at warming you up all inside! She seemed to love every-body and everybody seemed to love her. Lots of people loved to come to Grandpa and Grandma's farm.

Well, you had to be smart, you couldn't just gorge yourself with all those sweet Smores so Grandma had thought of something else that was re-ally neat to eat. She bought some cans of biscuit dough and showed them how to take out one biscuit dough. It was good to have a stick as big around as about the size of a quarter. You'd put the stick in the middle of the biscuit and wrap its sides around the stick. Now when you toasted that dough it would turn into the neatest little cup.

You'd slip your little cup off the end of the stick. You'd fill it with peanut butter or peanut butter and jelly. M-mm-mmm! That was sooo good! Thank you, Grandma, for thinking of such a great treat!

When everybody seemed to fill their tummies full of goodies Grandpa pulled up with his gray Ford tractor.

He'd hooked a big flat hay wagon onto the tractor. The wagon was full of loose hay. Everybody ran to get the best seat on the wagon and made their own little nest in the hay. The moms and dads warned their kids to find a safe place and not get so rowdy that they forgot to stay safe.

Grandpa always drove nice and slow down the gravel road. He loved hearing the kids laughing and even the big kids, especially Grandma.

Mikey tried to get Hound Dog to come up in the hay with him but nope, Hound Dog was going to trot along and keep an eye on where Grandpa was going.

There was a big moon shining brightly this night. There were lots of twinkling little stars but the kids didn't seem to be quiet enough to even notice the moon and stars. They were just having so much fun getting together again and riding along, out in the open, along the gravel road going where Grandpa wanted to go.

Every once in awhile a bush would reach out and swipe them as they went by and they thought that was fun. The moms and dads were listening to their kids laughing and had their own stories to tell of when they were a kid and on a hayride!

They hated to feel Grandpa turn around but it was getting late and they just couldn't keep going and going.

When Grandpa stopped the tractor everybody jumped off and thanked Grandma and Grandpa for such a fun day!

When they got home, you better believe it, before you knew it they were sound asleep! The moon could shine in their faces all it wanted to but they didn't even know it.

All the little creatures could tease Hound Dog with all their little chatter but this night Hound Dog was dead tired, too. He'd marched right along on that long walk today. And he'd trotted beside the hayride tonight. He loved having all those kids petting him and he'd ever been on alert to make sure he was protecting them and the farm.

Tomorrow would be another day for Mikey and Hound Dog to have another adventure.

Mikey and Hound Dog—they would be buddies forever! Just as Pougie grew up to be Hound Dog, Mikey would grow up to be Mitch, but they would always remember their growing-up days together on Grandpa's farm—best buddies forever!

We invite you to view the complete
selection of titles we publish at:
www.TEACHServices.com

scan with your mobile
device to go directly
to our website

Please write or email us your praises, reactions, or
thoughts about this or any other book we publish at:

TEACH Services, Inc.
PUBLISHING
www.TEACHServices.com • (800) 367-1844

P.O. Box 954
Ringgold, GA 30736

Info@TEACHServices.com

TEACH Services, Inc., titles may be purchased in bulk
for educational, business, fund-raising, or sales
promotional use. For information, please e-mail:

BulkSales@TEACHServices.com

Finally if you are interested in seeing
your own book in print, please contact us at

publishing@TEACHServices.com

We would be happy to review your manuscript for free.